Love and pain from a Muslim Mum

Sheema Ishaque

BookLeaf Publishing

India | USA | UK

Love and pain from a Muslim Mum © 2024
Sheema Ishaque

Presentation by *BookLeaf Publishing*

Web: www.bookleafpub.com

E-mail: info@bookleafpub.com

ISBN:9789358317350

First edition 2024

DEDICATION

I dedicate this to my family who I will forever fight for.

I am changed

Change, an unyielding force, woven into life's discourse,
Resisting it, a futile endeavor, as time charts its course.
People, like shifting shadows, alter views and stance,
Adapting to the rhythm, caught in the dance.

Accepting change, a daunting quest, an internal test,
How to perceive it as good, lay inner turmoil to rest?
In the midst of life's transformative swirl,
Questioning self, relationships, the unfolding world.

Amidst this metamorphic symphony, I stand,
A stranger to my former self, like shifting sand.
Wondering, is it solely my evolution's decree,
Or do others, too, undergo this profound journey?

The realization dawns, a potent truth,
No longer the doormat, forgiving uncouth.
Inner turmoil wrestles with the familiar role,

Should I mend as before, or embrace a new
goal?

But this time, a different resolve unfolds,
Prioritizing self, as the narrative unfolds.
No more the perpetual giver, endlessly kind,
Asking, "Why always me?" in the echoes of the
mind.

Embracing change, in self and in strife,
Seeing myself first, recalibrating life.
Understanding, what once seemed strange,
Is the emergence of a beautifully changed range.

As seasons change and winds rearrange,
Life's canvas extends, allowing for a longer
range.
In this symphony of evolution, I find,
A lengthened poem, a reflection of a shifting
mind.

Wake Up

Wake up to the silent abuse,
Not just physical; mental and financial, a subtle
ruse.
Years blind to the toll it takes,
Now, reality hits, illusions break.

Used and manipulated, a bitter revelation,
Kind acts, spent pennies, mere manipulation.
Building what I thought were bonds,
Realizing it was for nothing, beyond.

Stuck in a cycle with no clear end,
No escape, just echoes, wounds to mend.
A single plea echoes in the void,

Wake up!

Abuse wears many faces,
Not just physical embraces.
Mental strains, unseen scars,
A silent war behind closed doors.

Realize the truth, break the chains,
Kindness wasted, patience drained.
Love unreturned, a painful dance,

Redirect it, give yourself a chance.

Wake up, don't let it be in vain,
Break free from the silent pain.

I hate unicorns

In a world of unicorns and hues so pink,
Candy floss? To that, I squarely clink.

Fluffy socks and fairy wings, not my trend,
But in a monster outfit, bear-like growls ascend.

No Twinkle twinkle, no pixie dust,
Give me slime, gooey things, a must.

Sparkles and glitter, assail my eyes,
Seek refuge in dirt, where reality lies.

Sugar, spice, and niceties in a row,
Not for me, don't say it, let the truth show.

I loathe unicorns, detest all things pink,
Yet, still a girl, with thoughts that uniquely link.

The grind

In the ceaseless saga of the grind we endure,
Sleep, work, eat, a cycle obscure.
Counting down days with a repetitive beat,
When will the weekend bring a retreat?

Only five days, then four, three, and two,
The last day, a dull, monotonous view.
Woohoo for two, a fleeting cheer,
Yet the final day, a tedious frontier.

The weekend arrives, a brief reprieve,
Free time slipping away, like a thief.
Catching up, ticking chores with haste,
Resting briefly before the grind's next embrace.

For in this never-ending story we're bound,
Sleep, work, eat, the cycle profound.
Repeat echoes through each passing day,
In the relentless cadence of life's rhythmic play.

Healing

In the journey, my friend, ease finds its way,
The pain will dull, subsiding day by day.
Grief, a constant companion, never fully gone,
Yet in learning, in coping, in memories, we
dawn.

I held back tears, needed to be strong,
While others crumbled, I couldn't go wrong.
Better days emerge, the pain finds reprieve,
Lessening its grip, granting solace to believe.

It won't vanish, this ache in our core,
Yet in learning, in coping, in memories, we
implore.
Life unfolds with its intricate hues,
Living, loving, and, inevitably, losing cues.

I continued to live, demanded to be strong,
While tears cascaded where others belonged.
Time, they say, brings healing's embrace,
Though it lingers, an indelible trace.

Not complete, but softer it becomes,
In learning, in coping, life's symphony strums.
And as the clock ticks, memories endure,

We live, we love, and, in loss, we mature.

Love is unfinished

In the symphony of love, an endless melody,
With ups and downs, rounds that unfold freely.
Consuming, overwhelming, an emotion bold,
A beginning marked, but where does its story
hold?

For those who love, a blessing divine,
On and on, an infinite line.
Changing, evolving, a timeless dance,
Will this blessing of love forever enhance?

To love without return, a noble quest,
Give and take, a heart's earnest request.
Never take it for granted, for it may depart,
When lost, does love rekindle, a second start?

For all who love, an open-ended tune,
No conclusive end, beneath the moon.
It never halts, in constant rearranges,
Love, a story that perennially changes.

Love until it's unfinished, a continuum in grace,
A journey unbounded, an endless embrace.

Which one are you?

In every sphere, the cast is set,
Gossip guy, by the book, the one to fret.
Class bully, life and soul's blend,
Snitch, goody two shoes, the one to defend.

Bitchy vibes, too nice to be real,
Token Asian, token black, faces we feel.
Man about town, the one who slacks,
Cool for school, the rebel tracks.

In one year, out the other, they sway,
Corrupting others, leading them astray.
A spectrum diverse, more types to unveil,
Overlap exists, stories to tell.

Can you spot yourself in this array?
Any surprises, as roles come into play?
I know where I stand, which one I am,
In this dynamic ensemble, each has its jam.

From work to school, family to friends,
Who's the one with a motive that bends?
Awaiting the chance, poised to take,
In the intricate web, which role will you stake?

My Abu

My Abu is a funny dad

My Abu is a funny dad. He does lots of funny things.

His beard is long, it has white hairs, grey hairs and black hairs. He always tries to tickle my face with his beard. But I say you have to catch me first!

My Abu cycles to work and back. when he comes home he is always so smelly! He likes to give me smelly hugs! But I always run away and hide.

My Abu wears a lunghi at home. It's traditional Bangladeshi clothes for men. He looks so funny and he wears it outside! Sometimes I hide my face.

My Abu loves his laptop, he's always working on it. I love his laptop too and I can't help but tap away when he's not looking. One day he caught me typing so I told him I wrote him a letter. But I was only two!

My Abu loves to eat but he takes so long. I wait and wait for him to come a play but then I get bored!

My Abu is a funny dad, he always makes me laugh! He tells some funny jokes and stories. Sometimes I don't understand but he laughs so I laugh.

My Abu loves his car, I think more than he loves my mum. He spends forever cleaning it and my mum wonders where he went.

I love my Abu a lot, even though I pretend I don't. He's the funniest man I know. In the mornings I get into my parents bed and Abu gives me the biggest cuddle. This time I don't run away because Abu's cuddles are the best.

Letter to my unborn

In the realm of might-have-beens, you'd be my
number three,
Realizing love in loss, the depth I couldn't
foresee.
Different from the others, a unique part of me,
I ponder if I could have done more, a lingering
plea.

You felt safe, worry didn't haunt your space,
Yet, life unfolded, and God chose a different
trace.
Naive hopes, shattered by fate's decree,
Accepting now, you're in heaven, forever free.

The physical pain, a relentless wave,
Yet, the aftermath's emptiness, the heart couldn't
stave.
We'll meet someday, a promise profound,
Islam's solace, a truth beautifully crowned.

Rest, little one, in the realms above,
In my heart, wrapped in an eternal love.
A day will come when we'll never part,
Islam's grace, connecting us, heart to heart.

Love always, Mum.

Quiet

In the stillness of the night, a rare retreat,
Husband and kids in slumber deep.
Work awaits in the morning light,
Yet, the allure of silence takes flight.

Embracing the quiet, a tranquil space,
Thoughts echo, a serene embrace.
The mind, a movie with a voiceover's art,
In the hush, hearing each thought depart.

Such moments are scarce, noise ever near,
Life's symphony, constant and clear.
Quiet time usually reserved for sleep,
Yet, sometimes, elusive dreams to reap.

Now, a different hush, not sleep-induced,
A silence rare, a moment seduced.
Time standing still, a fleeting grace,
In this quietude, finding a peaceful place.

Breathing deeply, thoughts take flight,
For once, just being, in the quiet of the night.
A reminder of stillness, a cherished decree,
A moment in time when it's just you and me.

Forgive me

In the tender silence of forgiveness, we sway,
For the times you hit and were angry today.
No words spoken, yet love finds its way,
Cuddled before bed, a gentle, forgiving display.

For moments when attention seemed astray,
For getting angry, for leaving for work each day.
Little one, emotions big and hard to convey,
Tiny hands on my face, arms embracing, they
say.

You're too little for words, emotions undefined,
Navigating a world vast, intricate, and unlined.
In those embraces, in each heartfelt touch,
A language of love, expressing so much.

The unspoken forgiveness in the quiet night,
A bond unbroken, everything feeling right.
Sweetheart, you and I, learning day by day,
In cuddles and embraces, our emotions find a
way.

Letter to my eldest

My firstborn, a prayer answered, a cherished
delight,
Mummy loves you endlessly, morning, noon,
and night.
You're my superstar, shining bright,
Growing into a smart boy, a source of pure
delight.

Your articulate mind, a marvel to see,
Kind-hearted, distinguishing right from wrong,
so gracefully.
I'm proud of the person you're becoming,
With the wisdom and kindness, your heart is
humming.

You can achieve all you set your sight,
Give your best, my love, in every fight.
Be whatever you dream, pursue with zest,
Always striving, never settling for less.

A good person, kind-hearted, generous, and true,
These qualities, my dear, will see you through.
Look after your siblings, my wise little man,
Though it's tough, you were born to lead this
clan.

On your shoulders, responsibilities may seem,
Yet, you carry them with grace, a childhood
dream.
The nurses saw wisdom in your newborn eyes,
Defying odds, you're here, a beautiful surprise.

My eldest, a miracle, against the odds you stand,
A testament to strength, resilience grand.
You are loved, my blessing, my wise little man,
Forever my miracle, part of an extraordinary
plan.

Love you always,
Mum

Letter to my middle one

In tales of wildness, feral they say,
Lively and loud, in your vibrant display.
Stubborn, a trait they often find,
Yet, I see a spirit, uniquely kind.

From birth, a soul so gentle and sweet,
Compassion and consideration, your heartbeat.
At six, you comforted, amidst the wild,
Your kindness, my solace, my gentle child.

Feral and lively, oh, so loud,
But in your heart, a gentleness endowed.
Thoughtful and stubborn, forging your ways,
A strength that promises remarkable days.

In life's journey, you'll reach far and wide,
Oh, my child, with a spirit full of pride.
Love you always, in every style,
For the wild, the gentle, my feral wild child.

Love you always,
Mum

Letter to my baby

Baby, forever you are,
Time may pass, but never far.
From that twinkle to a cheeky grin,
You, my love, always within.

The way you talk, your negotiations keen,
I wonder, who in the world have you seen?
Then I realize, a blend so true,
A bit of me and much of your dad too.

Sweetest little boy, destined to grow,
Into the sweetest man, this I know.
You made us whole, a family of five,
In your laughter, our joy thrives.

Can't fathom life without your glee,
You, my baby, complete our family.
Keep smiling, my precious delight,
Forever my baby, in every light.

Love always,
Mum.

No hope

Reflecting on why, questioning belief,
Expectations shattered, causing grief.
Why, why, why, the perpetual cry,
Learning eludes me, a recurring sigh.

Angry at myself, for a slip-up's cost,
Knew better, know better, a lesson lost.
Yet, beneath it all, a glimmer of hope,
A yearning for change, a way to cope.

Hope whispers, "This time, a different tale,"
No more letdowns, no more to derail.
Yet here I am, drowning in sorrow,
Sadness, disappointment, anger to borrow.

It's clear now, the power lies within,
The choice is mine, where to begin.
No need to endure it all over again,
To break free from the cycle, the internal chain.

Observing you and the path ahead,
How it's been and what lies ahead.
Distinguishing hope, a daunting task,
Putting it out for good, no more to bask.

Is it human nature, this longing for hope?
A delicate thread we tightly grope.
Without hope, a surrender to despair,
Yet, not everything, I'm determined to declare.

I won't give up on everything, that's true,
But hope for change, I bid adieu.
No expectations, no hopeful gaze,
Accepting reality in life's intricate maze.

Hijab

In the ritual of leaving, Hijab unfolds,
A scarf, a shield, as the story's told.

Wrapped around her head, a careful twirl,
"What's that sharp thing, Ammu?" I ask, a
curious swirl.

"It's a pin," she responds, securing the attire,
"To keep it in place," she adds with a smile so
entire.

"Does it hurt, Ammu?" my innocent plea,
"It doesn't touch my head, just the fabric, you
see."

Finishing the ritual, a glance in the mirror,
"Perfect!" she says, her demeanor clearer.

"Why wear it, Ammu?" my question so keen,
"The Quran guides, modesty is the sheen.
Women cover their beauty, for husbands to
unveil,To guard and cherish, the essence of the
tale."

"Oh, that's why when you go out," I realize,

"Exactly," she nods, a truth that implies.

"When I grow up, a Hijab I'll don too,"
I declare, wrapping a scarf, as if on cue.

Mummy takes my head, her hands gently
pressed,
"Ma Sha Allah, beautiful," her words, a loving
zest.

Ball of Red

Walking to school, a moaning behind,
Scary sounds, but looking, I'm confined.
Mummy warns, "Don't look!" in a hurry,
Louder it grows, my curiosity does worry.

Turning back, a glimpse I seek,
A ball of red with big eyes, not meek.
Mum insists, "Don't give attention, don't delay,"
But it's saying something, I want to hear what
it'll say.

"Diyayso scaf, diyaso scaf," it growls,
Words unfamiliar, a language that prowls.
Tiny eyes in windows, curious stares,
Wondering, "What's making those monster
flares?"

Mum ushers, "Hurry up, don't be late,"
"Diyaso, Diyaso," the monster's fate.
Shouting, screaming, as we reach my classroom
door,
People stare, some ignore, others explore.

"Diyaso scaaaaaaaaaf," it screams in a roar,

Mum waits, the ball of red, not a monster
anymore.
Bending down, she cuddles with care,
My little sister Rara, the source of the scare.

A dinosaur scarf, that's what she lacked,
The bright red coat, the monster unpacked.
Mum turns to me, a lesson well done,
"Well done for keeping your things on," she says
with a pun.

Shoe monster

"Ouch!" exclaimed Mum, stumbling on a
misplaced shoe,
She calls to Rara, "Put them away, the whole
shoe crew!"

Ten minutes later, another shoe dance,
"Tidy up, Rara, give these shoes a chance."

Dad, organizing the living room with precision,
Thuds to the floor, caught in a shoe collision.
"Rara, shoes away now!" his command, a
decision.

Mum sighs, eyeing Rara's shoe empire,
"Too many shoes, it's a saga that won't tire."
A shoe monster born, a quirky desire.

In the kitchen, both parents cook with care,
Mum suddenly screams, caught in a shoe scare.
Dad rushes over, "What's the matter?" he
inquires.

"Shooe shooe monster!" Mum plays the fear,
There's Rara, adorned in shoes, drawing near.
"I'm the shoe monster, catch me!" she cheers.

Hold on tight

In a difficult relationship, once so tight,
Now no win, once joined at the hip's plight.
Troubled times, problems begin,
Not wanting it like this, can it be given in?

Mended or forever bended,
Broken, tormented, a bond upended.
Wanting to do more, revert to days of yore,
A history hard to forget, now filled with lies
galore.

Fighting, arguing, armors are up,
Defending oneself, putting up a fuss, the bitter
cup.
Hard to go back, the question rings,
Only moving forward, can we mend the springs?